# The star party

written by
Noelle Yaney Child

illustrated by
Mariano Epelbaum

Richmond

Today is Rachel's birthday and she is celebrating it with her family at Paolo's Pizzeria.

'Thank you for the pizza,' said Rachel when they were leaving the restaurant. 'Next year, could you please not sing? It's embarrassing. I'm eleven, not four!'

Her mother and father laughed.

Rachel climbed into the back seat next to her younger sister, Alyssa. Alyssa's birthday was last week. Both Rachel and Alyssa did not like having August birthdays.

Every August most of their friends go away. Some go on family holidays and others go to camp. No one is there for parties.

'I need to make a stop before going home, okay?' said Rachel's dad.

'Okay,' said Rachel. Alyssa gave her a magazine and they began to read. Almost half an hour later, Rachel looked up. They had driven out of town.

'Where are you going?' asked Rachel.

'Almost there,' said Rachel's father. Alyssa asked Rachel for help with a crossword puzzle. Fifteen minutes later, Rachel's father stopped the car at the entrance of a national park. There were lots of cars there.

'Surprise!' said Rachel's parents. 'You said you wanted to go camping this summer, didn't you?' asked Alyssa, smiling.

'A campout? Cool!' said Rachel.

'It's a star party that dad and I heard about on the radio,' said Alyssa.

'What is a star party?' Rachel asked.

'You'll see.'

The family set up their tent at the edge of a big field and went to explore the campsite. The field was filled with tents. People were setting up telescopes everywhere. Some were small telescopes, others were taller than Rachel!

As night fell, someone rang a bell in the centre of the field. People went and waited around an exceptionally big telescope. A man named Mr Wexler welcomed everyone to the Rock Park Annual Star Party. He was an astronomer from the Murdock Planetarium.

'I'd like to tell everyone a little about tonight's big event: the Perseid meteor shower,' said Mr Wexler. 'The Perseid shower happens every year around the 11th of August. This is when planet Earth passes through a trail of debris in space.

The debris was left by the comet Swift-Turtle. Swift-Turtle only orbits the Sun about every 130 years. It also leaves enough comet dust till its next visit.'

'The comet's debris is made up of very small particles of rock and dust. Most are about the size of a grain of sand. These particles crash into the Earth's atmosphere at a speed of 212,000 km/h, causing them to burn up. This is what produces the bright streaks of light that we call meteors.'

‘We’ll see meteors when the Sun sets. The biggest showers will happen between 2.00 a.m. and dawn.’

The sky began to darken as Mr Wexler continued talking. He explained the rules of the star party. He asked everyone to keep the campsite clean. He told people to be respectful. He said the quiet hours would be between midnight and 7.00 a.m.

Then, Mr Wexler explained light pollution.

'Can you see that glow in the western horizon? It's caused by the city lights. The glow in the sky is not too bright out here in the park. However, it'll limit the stars we can see. Some stargazers travel far to find places with very dark skies. There, they can see thousands more stars and meteors.'

Mr Wexler asked everyone to turn off their lights at the star party. 'Only use torches covered with a red filter. Using red lights helps reduce glare. Glare is light that keeps our eyes from adjusting to the dark. Glare makes it difficult to see stars even with a telescope. I have tape and red plastic for anyone who needs them.' Rachel and Alyssa covered their torches.

Back at the tent, Rachel's parents gave them chairs to sit on. They introduced the girls to their camp neighbours, Mr and Mrs Duncan. The Duncans told the family all about the Amateur Astronomy Club.

'You should come to one of our monthly stargazing sessions. Most of us just enjoy stargazing, but a few of our members are serious about astronomy. Last year one member discovered a new star. Professional astronomers are studying the star now.'

Finally, the sky was dark. At first, Rachel could only see a few stars in the sky. Mr Duncan pointed out Venus, above the horizon. Slowly, more stars and planets appeared.

'Ohhhh!' everyone in the field said at the sight of the first big meteor. For one moment, you could see its wide trail across the sky. Then it slowly disappeared.

'An Earthgrazer!' exclaimed someone.

'You'll only see a few of those,' said Mrs Duncan.

Rachel's family saw one more Earthgrazer and many small meteors. Then, they went around the field taking turns to use different telescopes. One amateur astronomer showed them the rings around Saturn. Another showed them the moons of Jupiter. Mr Wexler pointed his big telescope towards several objects in outer space.

'I can't believe we saw a real nebula!' said Rachel's father on their way back to the tent.

Around half past ten, Rachel's mother told the girls to sleep a little. She promised to wake them for the most active part of the meteor shower. Soon their mother was waking them up. It was 4.00 a.m. and it was very dark. They got up sleepily and looked at the sky.

'Wow!' Rachel and Alyssa said.

'What is all that white stuff in the middle of the sky? Is that meteor dust?' asked Alyssa.

'It's the Milky Way,' said Rachel's mother. 'It's what we can see of our galaxy. The white stuff is made up of a billion distant stars. We can't see the Milky Way at home because there's too much light pollution in town.'

'Look at all the meteors. They're falling everywhere.' said Rachel. She and Alyssa lay down on their backs and watched in silence.

Meteors striped the black sky. Looking up at the Milky Way, Rachel thought about Earth's place in the galaxy. Watching the meteors, she could almost feel herself flying through space. She was nothing more than a small creature on a small rock in the universe.

'August birthdays are the best!' said Alyssa.

'Yes, it's true!' smiled Rachel.